CURRENT AFRICAN ISSUES 56

I0122940

Election-Related Violence:
The Case of Ghana

Clementina Amankwaah

NORDISKA AFRIKAINSTITUTET, UPPSALA 2013

INDEXING TERMS:
Ghana
Elections
Electoral systems
Voting
Political violence
Ethnicity
Politics
Political parties
Democracy

ISSN 0280-2171
ISBN 978-91-7106-744-9
Language editing: James Middleton
© The author and the Nordic Africa Institute
Production: Byrå4
Print on demand. Lightning Source UK Ltd.

Contents

Introduction 5

Methodological approach 9

Case study findings 10
   Politics, chieftaincy and revenge: the case of Tamale/Yendi 10
   Narratives of Tamale/Yendi elections 11
   Ethnicity and party politics: the case of Kumasi.....................................18
   Macho men 21
   Narratives of Kumasi elections...22
   The case of Greater Accra 26
   Instability in employment: the civil service and business people in Accra.............28

Concluding remarks 31
   Causes of violence 31
   Perpetrators of violence 32
   The role of big men in violence..32

References 33

Appendix 1 35

This background paper is an introductory overview of the causes and experiences of election-related violence in relation to patronage politics in Ghana. Ghana has been framed by the international community as a unique bastion of democracy and peace on the African continent. Nevertheless, the country has come from a military regime like many of its democratic African counterparts and is still prone to some of the problems faced by its more turbulent neighbours (Utas, 2012b). Mansfield and Snyder (2007) observe an upsurge in violence rather than a decrease when countries in transition undergo elections.

Although the pockets of violence during election time in Ghana may be comparatively less severe than in many other countries on the continent, to ignore incidents that occur during elections is also possibly to ignore the symptoms for potential explosions of violence later (Jockers, Kohnert and Nugent, 2009). The interviewees in this paper confirm that they felt that the December 2008 elections were extremely tense and marred by more violence across the country than usual, though the December 2012 election was one of the most peaceful the country has seen in the past eight years[1].

If Ghana really is a consolidated democracy, then the way that electoral fraud is dealt with and investigated should test this. However, this did not happen in 2008 when complaints about electoral fraud from and about the country's two largest parties, the National Democratic Congress (NDC) and the New Patriotic Party (NPP), were not investigated. Jockers, Kohnert and Nugent (2009) speculated that the electoral commission (EC) may have not wanted to "open a can of worms" or perhaps did not have the time or money to investigate the complaints.

The international community also needed to maintain Ghana's image as an African example of peace for other, less democratic African countries to follow (2009). In 2012, the NPP rejected the 2012 election results, complaining of electoral fraud. The party is currently pursuing its grievances in court. In the media, some argued that, in the interest of peace, the NPP should simply accept the results the EC had declared and not take the matter further. However, the test of democracy must be performed in other ways than through elections alone (Hennemeyer, 2011).

Others have argued that a country's judicial system is just as important in determining whether a country is democratic or not: it is the NPP's right to take its grievances to court because a country can never be democratic without also ensuring justice (Diedong, 2012). No matter the outcome of the court case, the

---

1. The national elections held in 2004 and 2008 were considerably more violent than the elections held in 2012.

fact that many have argued that the issue should be left alone suggests that some Ghanaians perceive peace in Ghana as relatively fragile.

Hence a study of people's experiences and perceptions of violence because of elections in Ghana is not only important to understand how and why violence occurs in the country, but also how people try to preserve peace. As a highly understudied area in Ghana, the international community cannot take elections and peace for granted if many Ghanaians themselves are not confident that country-wide peace is the norm.

How are Ghanaians' voting patterns related to violence during elections? If we focus on voting patterns since the first democratic elections in Ghana in 1996, Lindberg and Morrison (2005) found that only approximately 10% of Ghanaian voters who responded to a survey reported that they had voted for candidates for clientelist or ethno-regional reasons in that year. The number of respondents who voted for these reasons rose to 14% in 2000. Lindberg and Morrison interpreted the voting patterns of people in NPP and NDC strongholds as likely to be because of "legacies resulting in a political socialization". Moreover:

> "A study carried out in the Techiman southern constituency after the 1996 election also indicates that socialization through family and peers plays a crucial role in reproducing voter alignments but does not indicate an ethnic component to this."
> (p.113)

However, two of the respondents in this study from the Ashanti region (the main NPP stronghold) stated that the NPP are seen as an Akan/Ashanti party; if you told people that you voted for the NDC and they knew that you were Akan, they would think you were stupid, crazy or a traitor. Whether people admit to voting for reasons unrelated to ethnicity and clientelism or not, the Ashanti and Volta regions have consistently voted for the NPP and NDC respectively since the first elections in 1992 (Jockers, Kohnert and Nugent, 2009).

The northern regions (Upper East, Upper West and Northern regions) have all also consistently voted for the NDC since Ghana's first elections, though the NPP gained a lot of ground in 2000. People from the southern cities of Kumasi and Accra, where elections are less related to chieftaincy, said that election-related violence occurred most often in ethnically heterogeneous areas. However, a study of where violence occurred shows that it was commonly in strongholds of political parties where political minority groups also lived. For example, NDC members who are jubilant over the President John Dramani Mahama's victory could be verbally and sometimes physically attacked in the NPP's Kumasi stronghold.

In Ghana, Greater Accra, Western, Central and Brong Ahafo are regions with a high number of swing voters. They all voted for presidential power to change hands from the NDC to the NPP in 2000 and for the NPP to maintain its power in 2004. However, in 2008 the NDC won in the Greater Accra and Central regions in the first round. In the run-off, all four of the swing regions voted for the NDC. Lindberg and Morrison (2005) found that swing voters in Ghana stated reasons less related to clientelism and ethnicity and more related to political issues for their voting choices.

In Ghana, elections have been relatively calm in comparison to elections in neighbouring West African countries. However, it has been difficult to ascertain much detail on election-related violence in Ghana as a whole, because media reports of incidents of violence are often scant, with few studies prioritising the matter in research. Nevertheless, the main conclusion that most media reports and research into elections and violence in Ghana since 1992 have drawn is that pockets of violence often occur in certain parts of the country, though the amount of reports of violence can vary from year to year.

For example, many experienced the presidential elections of 2012 as peaceful compared to the previous elections of 2008 and 2004. Why was this? Interviewees for this paper gave several reasons. Firstly, the competition between the two candidates in 2012 was not as close as it had been in the 2008 election when there had been a run-off[2]. It seems that the combination of a close competition and an extended election process were factors that heightened tension in the 2008 elections.

Adolfo et al. (2012) state that:

> *"Winning an election may be a matter of survival for the competing parties, as well as for entire communities within the state. The risk of electoral violence may therefore be higher in situations where there is real political competition between various parties and genuine possibilities to change existing power relations. All elections involve elements of uncertainty, but if the winner takes all, the uncertainties of democracy come at a high price."*

The political competition between the two candidates was the keenest during the period between the first round and run-off of the 2008 election. This was also the time when the NPP and the NDC used young men to snatch ballot boxes and intimidate voters in opposition strongholds around the country.

Another factor that has led to election-related violence in Ghana is when either the NPP or the NDC are tied to factions that dispute chieftaincy rights. This has been the case in northern towns such as Yendi and Bawku because the possibility of gaining chieftaincy rights is directly related to whether or not a

---

2. In December 2008, the NPP's Nana Akuffo-Addo received 49.77% of the vote, and the late president John Evans Atta-Mills won with 50.23%. In December 2012, Akuffo-Addo received 47.74% of votes and John Dramani Mahama of the NDC won with 50.70% (National Electoral Commission). Despite the small margin of difference, people saw this gap as a significant one compared to 2008, especially as there was no run-off, which led to less tension.

faction's preferred party wins elections. At no point in the interviews or discussions I had were any of the smaller parties identified as violent. This is perhaps because competition has never been keen among these parties. None of them have ever received even 1% of votes for the presidency.

The three main guiding issues that this background paper will address in relation to election-related violence in Ghana are:

- The causes of election-related violence in Ghana
- Who the people most likely to cause election-related violence are and how often they do this
- The role that "big men" play in election-related violence

The paper presents brief case studies of areas spanning three regions in Ghana. These areas are among the most commonly cited flashpoints for election-related violence in the country. The capital of Northern region Tamale, the third-largest city in Ghana, and nearby Dagbon capital Yendi[3]; Kumasi, Ghana's second city, which is in Ashanti region; and the capital Accra in Greater Accra region (see Figure 1 map below).

I carried out fieldwork over the course of nearly two weeks, travelling between the three locations. However, because of the long distances involved and the fact that the fieldwork had to be undertaken over the Christmas and New Year period (when respondents were less available to meet and offices were not always open), the actual fieldwork duration was approximately seven days. Two days in Tamale, one in Yendi, two in Kumasi and two in Accra. The method I used was mainly unstructured interviews and casual conversations.

Figure 1 Map of Ghana (UN Cartographic Section)

---

3. I studied these two locations as one unit because I would argue that in relation to the Yendi conflict and within elections, the city of Tamale almost acts as a satellite city to the small town of Yendi. This will be further discussed in the paper below.

Politics, chieftaincy and revenge: the case of Tamale/Yendi

Yendi is a small town, approximately 2.5 hours' drive from the capital of Northern region Tamale. Tamale and Yendi are in the area of Dagbon, the homeland of the Dagomba ethnic group. Although parts of Dagbon are heterogeneous, Tamale in particular, the Dagomba are, nevertheless the largest ethnic group in Northern region[4]. Yendi is the capital of Dagbon, where the *Ya-Naa* (paramount chief of Dagbon) resides.

The NDC often wins legislative and presidential elections across the three northern regions (Northern, Upper West and Upper East). However, among the Dagomba an intra-ethnic feud has ensued in one royal family since the 19th century. This feud led the Dagomba to split into the Abudu and Andani branches of the royal family, which Dagombas refer to as "gates". Abudu and Andani were sons of paramount chief Ya-Naa Yakubu I by different mothers (Abudu's mother was Ya-Naa Yakubu's first wife and Andani's mother the chief's second wife) who were "enskinned"[5] in succession during the 1800s. A complicated series of events developed after Ya-Naa Andani died in 1899, which eventually led to Dagbon splitting between the Andani and Abudu gates.

Even though Ya-Naa Yakubu had many other children with other wives, the majority of Dagombas identify themselves with either the Ya-Naa Abudu or Ya-Naa Andani line today[6]. Competition between the two gates is fierce because the Dagomba practice a winner-takes-all system of rule, whereby the man enskinned as paramount chief in Yendi can also enskin his family members and supporters into most of the other sub-chief positions in Dagbon (Ibrahim, 2012; Weiss, 2005, p.7).

To gain powerful political support for their chieftaincy dispute today the Abudus generally support the NPP and the Andanis have rallied around the NDC. The combination of kin-based feud and political division is why confrontations between NDC and NPP supporters in the northern region are also often between members of the Andani and Abudu gates. Yet the support for the two

---

4. According to the Ghanaian census of 2010, the Tamale metropolitan area had a population of 371,351, whereas Yendi's population totaled 199,592 people. The Mole-Dagbani ethnic group was the largest in Northern region in 2010 at 1,258,657 people. The Gurma group followed, with 651,088 people (Ghana Statistical Service, 2012).

5. In Dagbon, a new chief sits on a set of cow skins when he comes to power, thus when a chief gains his position, he is said to be enskinned.

6. It is not within the scope of this paper to explain the complicated history of the Abudu and Andani split in Dagbon.

biggest political parties from the Dagombas and the traditions the parties have come from have been apparent since independence[7].

The main preoccupation for each gate is to support either the NPP or NDC and help that party win power to settle the Dagomba chieftaincy dispute to the gate's advantage. For example, an Andani interviewee in Tamale explained that in exchange for voting for the NDC, the party will ensure that the Andani Ya-Naa remains enskinned in Yendi and is not killed or overthrown by the Abudu gate as the interviewee believed had occurred in the conflict of 2002. Chieftaincy support in exchange for political support from Andani votes for the NDC operates similarly between the Abudus and the NPP.

In March 2002, Andani paramount chief Ya-Naa Yakubu Andani II (Yakubu) was killed in Yendi on the final day of a three-day conflict between the Abudu and Andani gates. The NPP under the presidency of John Kufuor (2001–2009) had been in government for 15 months. The cause of the chief's death is mysterious and still has not been confirmed. Stories about the conflict abound, but the most widely reported version of events was that he was beheaded[8]. According to the Andani gate, national politics entered the local war when the army sent men on the orders of the NPP government to fight on behalf of the Abudus and kill the Dagbon chief.

Narratives of Yendi/Tamale elections

The first person I spoke with in Tamale about the Yendi conflict was a young Andani man who did not want to be identified or associated with the study at all. When I asked him what had happened in Yendi, while checking around the bar where we were drinking for possible listeners, he quietly replied that we should speak later when fewer people were around. When we were finally alone in the bar, he explained that on the first day of the Yendi conflict, people had been getting reports in Tamale that the Abudus were attacking the paramount chief.

Some Andani men from Tamale had quickly organised themselves and travelled to Yendi to defend their chief by the second day of fighting. What was puzzling to the Andani fighters was that they were not only conflict Abudus, but also men in military uniforms, suggesting that they were actually fighting

---

7. The NDC come from the socialist tradition of the Convention People's Party (CPP). The NDC took inspiration from the president of Gold Coast and first president of Ghana Kwame Nkrumah (1951–66) and later shaped themselves into a social democratic party. The NPP openly declare that they come from the Busia-Danquah, right-of-centre United Party (UP) tradition. The Andanis rallied around Nkrumah and the CPP following independence and would later support the NDC party that came from it. Conversely, the Abudus have supported the UP and the NPP that would later be created out of the UP.

8. An Abudu interviewee said he thought that Yakubu had been shot, whereas on a different occasion an Andani interviewee explained that the Ya-Naa could not have been shot by Abudu gunmen due to his great spiritual powers. The gunmen instead had to encircle Ya-Naa Yakubu tightly in order to hold him still, whilst others twisted and broke his neck.

the Ghanaian army. Moreover, all the phone lines had stopped working and the NPP government had sent no official security force of any kind to try and stop the conflict. The only national forces sent were in fact fuelling the conflict by fighting the Andanis themselves. By day three of the violence, Ya-Naa Yakubu Andani II had been killed.

The interviewee explained how the Andanis concluded that this was a government-backed assassination attempt by the Abudus in exchange for political support for the NPP in the 2004 presidential elections. This idea was reinforced when I interviewed two other Andanis in Yendi. Nevertheless, this idea was denied in a written statement made by the Abudu family to the Wuaku Commission that investigated the circumstances leading up to the chief's death (Abudu Family, n.d.; cited in Hughes, 2003). This promise of votes two years before elections is why I consider the conflict an example of election-related violence outside of an election year.

However, an NPP district assembly man who was also a well-known member of the Abudu gate commented in interview that it was in fact the Andani who had started the conflict by sending fighters from Tamale to attack the Abudus in Yendi. A tank had allegedly been found at the paramount chief's palace and no evidence existed to prove that the Ghanaian army had ever been at the scene in Yendi at all.

Although the violence took place in Yendi, events in Tamale are inextricably tied to what happens in Yendi and should arguably also be researched. The Yendi fighting is one of few examples of a conflict in a small, rural place that has had a big impact on a large urban setting. Following the Yendi conflict, in 2002 Tamale and Yendi were put under a curfew for two and a half years. Following the 2011 acquittal of 15 Abudu men who stood trial for the killing of Yakubu, Tamale and Yendi were put under a week's curfew after Andani youths set the NDC's Northern Region office on fire and vandalised the NDC's Tamale Central Constituency office. The two offices were located in the Tamale metropolis.

The NDC party, led by John Evans Atta-Mills, was in power at the time and Andani youths felt that they had not been given justice for the killing of their paramount chief. My interviewee, a young man from Tamale, said that in a bid to appease the Andani youths and bring them back into the NDC, the party used its political largesse to distribute items such as farm tractors, tools and money among the ringleaders. The Yendi conflict was related to the very specific objective of killing the chief. Since then, violence during and outside of elections has been a much rarer occurrence in Yendi, where everybody knows everybody else. This is less the case in Tamale, where anonymity in the large city is increased and the likelihood of being caught when a crime is committed is lower.

The Abudu/Andani feud is still an extremely sensitive topic. Among the six people I asked about the feud, in interviews or casual conversation, only one felt comfortable speaking about it in a public setting. Three of the six confessed that they were not comfortable speaking about it where we were at that time and that I should wait so that we could talk about it somewhere more private, because anybody could be listening.

Tension and sensitivity still surround the topic because the matter has not been settled. In contrast, following the 10-year Sierra Leonean war, which also ended decade ago, a major reconciliation effort helped to relieve tensions, making it easier for people to talk about the war. No comparable effort to reconcile people in Yendi has been made, just as the matter of who should succeed the murdered Ya-Naa has still not been agreed upon between the two gates. Thus an explosion of violence is possibly never far below the surface, either during or outside of election time.

The 2012 election year in Northern region was relatively peaceful, which surprised people in many areas of the country. Parts of the region with chieftaincy disputes such as in Yendi, and in Bawku in Upper East region, often experience most conflict during elections, yet the few incidents that occurred in 2012 seemed to take place in the south (e.g. Accra and Kumasi). In conversation with the Tamale police public relations officer (PRO), he told me that there were no reports of physical violence during the 2012 election process. This is against a background of highly tense and sometimes violent elections in 2004 and 2008.

There was, however, one incident of a "macho man"[9] snatching a biometric voter registration machine near the central market in Aboabo. The PRO stated that the would-be thief dumped the machine as he was being pursued by voters and disappeared. The voters carried the machine back to the polling station. The macho man was still at large at the time of my interview with the PRO on 3 December 2012.

To get a more detailed history of Dagbon and its relation to politics from an Abudu perspective, I interviewed Umaru Ibrahim,[10] a district assembly member in one of the NPP's strongholds in Northern region and also a spokesman for the Abudu gate. Mr Ibrahim is a teacher, with an almost encyclopaedic knowledge of Dagomba chieftaincy history and its inextricable links with national politics. He described himself as a *politician with a lineage with the NPP and for that matter the Abudu Gate.* Mr Ibrahim is a staunch NPP member and his narrative is useful because it shines a light on the experiences of a member of one of the big national parties in a region where the party is in the minority. As stated above, minorities in political party strongholds are the kinds of people who often experience violence and threats during elections in Ghana.

After giving a very detailed account of the history of the Yendi feud, we

---

9. A well-built man hired by politicians to disrupt elections and intimidate voters.
10. All names have been changed to protect the identities of interviewees.

moved onto Mr Ibrahim's experiences of election-related violence as an NPP man living in an NDC-dominated region. He began by talking about two NPP men who had been "clubbed to death" at polling stations in NDC strongholds during the 2004 presidential election. The majority of the interviews and reported cases of violence in Ghana suggest that election-related violence often occurs in areas that are strongholds of one of the two larger parties, where minority supporters can easily be intimidated. This is unlike the situation in a country such as in Sierra Leone, where very large groups of supporters from the two biggest parties may have street brawls during elections (Christensen and Utas, 2008; 533).

The first man Mr Ibrahim spoke about was the NPP chairman of the Kumbungu constituency. The chairman sat at the polling station as an observer. Mr Ibrahim said that the 2004 elections were "too hot! You couldn't dare ask any questions." Mr Ibrahim admitted that he did not know the details of what precisely led to fighting at the polling station, but when the chairman asked questions a fight started that resulted in a group of NDC supporters beating him unconscious.

Nevertheless, there were other NDC supporters at the polling station who tried to defend the chairman and carried him to the palace of the chief in the area. The chairman subsequently died of his injuries. Everybody in the village was too scared to testify who had clubbed the man to death, though there were many witnesses at the polling station.

The temperature was "hot" because Yakubu had been killed two years before and no suspects had been brought to book for it. Mr Ibrahim felt that the Andanis/NDC were particularly violent against the Abudus/NPP because they had lost their Andani Chief.

> UI[11]: *"At that time, the death of the Ya-Naa was too much in people, the passion was there, so in areas where Abudus were strong, had the majority, you wouldn't see these things because they were not in the aggrieved side."*
>
> CA[12]: *"You felt like it was revenge?"*
>
> UI: *"It was a revenge!"*

Though the murder of Yakubu had happened two years before the 2004 elections, the chairman's killers got away with his murder specifically during the election period. In many cases in West Africa, the election period is a window wherein violent party supporters can be protected by powerful politicians. Crimes that would be punished at other times are often left unpunished during election time. This is particularly the case when the party of the perpetrators

---

11. Umaru Ibrahim
12. Clementina Amankwaah

of violence wins power. Thus, when masked as election-related, violence can be used to "settle older scores" (Utas, 2012b). In short, the election period can be used as a particular window of time for the "world to turn upside down".

This window often opens within a political system when the fight for succession makes things less stable. The idea has been discussed in relation to other parts of Africa (Dirks, 1988), as well as in northern Ghana (Drucker-Brown, 1999). Dirks labelled the phenomenon "annual rituals of conflict" and considered it an integral part of the political system. I would tentatively suggest that parts of democratic elections in some new African democracies could very loosely be interpreted as such an annual ritual of conflict in that contests of succession are a time for grievances to be avenged and violence to be excused and go unpunished.

During election years, powerful patrons have also protected those with influential contacts for apolitically motivated acts such as petty crime. Mr Ibrahim described an event that started at a school park (playground) about five-minutes walk from his home during the early months of the 2008 election year. A young man knocked on Mr Ibrahim's door one night and told Mr Ibrahim that some men had chased him out of the park.

The young man had gone to Mr Ibrahim's house because he was a community leader. Mr Ibrahim then called some young men and went with them to the park. At the park, Mr Ibrahim and his men hid in various places, while one of his young men walked through the park pretending he was speaking to somebody on a mobile (cellular) phone. Mr Ibrahim and his group lay in ambush for the perpetrators. Three men quickly walked over to the man with the phone, hit him and tried to take his phone.

Mr Ibrahim's men jumped out of their hiding places and pounced on the three attackers, and wanted to kill them because they viewed the men as thieves. During the commotion, Mr Ibrahim's men were also calling out to Mr Ibrahim "Assembly man! Assembly man!" Mr Ibrahim knew that if the three men were killed then his name would be made public, so he got a few of his men to protect the now injured men and take them to the police.

They spoke to the patrol chief at the police station. The three men were interviewed and they gave three different explanations why they had been in the park. The three men were detained that night. At 6a.m. at Mr Ibrahim's house the next morning, he was surprised to receive a visit from his football colleague, who had also brought the regional NDC chairman with him. Mr Ibrahim said that the chairman was also a chief, a freedom fighter and like an older brother to him.

The chairman told Mr Ibrahim that he had been putting up a building in the park and that his "boys" (the men who had been arrested) were his watchmen, so they were not doing anything bad. Mr Ibrahim replied "I caught them red-handed, they were beating somebody." Mr Ibrahim said that the chairman begged Mr Ibrahim to release his boys and Mr Ibrahim eventually agreed that he would go to the police station.

The chairman then left. In sending a person that Mr Ibrahim admired and with whom he had a good relationship, this part of Mr Ibrahim's story illustrates the carrot method that the NDC used to sway Mr Ibrahim (from a minority party in Northern region) into doing what the party wanted him to do. Although it was not a financial reward as carrots may often be, it was reward enough for Mr Ibrahim to please a man who was like his "older brother".

Nevertheless, soon after the NDC chairman had left Mr Ibrahim's house, a neighbour arrived and told Mr Ibrahim that a group of NDC supporters were at the police station where the three suspects were being held, waiting to attack him. Mr Ibrahim then sent his own young NPP men to the scene before he went to "push" the NDC crowd back from the police entrance so that he could enter. When Mr Ibrahim arrived at the station he asked the police to release the three men.

Mr Ibrahim, however, advised the police that they should not release the men at that police station because tensions were too high, and that they should be released at an alternative station. Mr Ibrahim went with them and reached an agreement with the police to release the men on bail. The police at the alternative station told Mr Ibrahim that the police commander had wanted to see him the next day. At this point in the story Mr Ibrahim said to me "I want you also to see how police and politicians help to enflame passions and emotions of our youth and the rank and file."

The next day at the police station, before Mr Ibrahim saw the commander, a police inspector told him to be careful because the commander had already spoken with some NDC members of Parliament (MPs) before he had arrived. Mr Ibrahim was then taken to a room where the commander and the three arrested men were seated. The commander asked Mr Ibrahim why he had told people to beat the three men up. Mr Ibrahim replied that he had not. The three men had attacked somebody else and the youths overpowered them. He had tried to protect the three men because people were calling out his name, and he sent them to the police station.

> UI: *"He [the police commander] said 'What happened?' I said 'Someone had run to me to tell me that they had chased him out of the park, so I mobilised people.' He said 'Oh stop! Why did you mobilise people?' I 'shouldn't talk again.' The Police Commander! So I was charged! Then I have to call for them to come and bail me. So they had a fixed day for court. That's what police do! They listen to the politicians and turn the case against you!"*

The crimes of the three men had nothing to do with politics, yet their case of petty crime became embroiled in a political issue, where threats of violence and police charges suddenly became a reality for Mr Ibrahim. This story is an illustration of how "big men" are "nodes in networks, combining efforts in projects of joint action" (Utas 2012a: 1). A series of NDC big men with links to the three arrested men combined efforts to round up angry young men at the police station, manoeuvre Mr Ibrahim and the police into releasing their "boys" and charging their political opponents with a crime all within the space of two days.

They first used the carrot method[13] by getting the NDC Chairman to ask Mr Ibrahim to release his men. Then, despite the fact that Mr Ibrahim agreed to have the men bailed, they still used the stick by getting an angry mob to wait for him outside the police station ready to attack him unless their boys were released and having charges pressed against him.

We spoke further about Mr Ibrahim's experiences as a minority political group leader in the north, and his experiences of the 2012 election year. He explained that at least five NPP members were either physically attacked or nearly physically attacked at local radio stations for things they had said on air. Mr Ibrahim did not have the details of what had happened in 2012, but a group of NDC supporters had also nearly attacked him. I asked Mr Ibrahim what had happened in his own case. He began by explaining that Andanis always bring up the chieftaincy issue to "make the temperature high" when you are explaining political issues well.

Radio North Star is a local radio station which was owned by the late NPP vice-president of Ghana, Alieu Mahama (2004-08) when he was alive. Mr Ibrahim was part of a radio panel composed of two NPP members and two NDC members discussing political issues a few weeks after Atta-Mills and the NDC had won the presidential election in 2008 after a heated run-off. One of the NDC panellists, who was an Andani, stated that in all of Andani history since Ya-Naa Andansirli, Andanis had never been in a war and run away.

Mr Ibrahim replied that he was not presenting the facts correctly. Just because Ya-Naa Andansirli's name had Andani in it, it did not mean that he was an Andani. It was not possible that Ya-Naa Andansirli was Andani because there was never an Andani/Abudu split between Dagombas at the time of his reign. After Ya-Naa Andansirli died, nine more chiefs would be enskinned before Abudu, then Andani, came into office. After this comment Mr Ibrahim said that NDC supporters had come to the radio station with chains and sticks to attack him. Luckily he and the other NPP panellist were shown a secret room to hide in as NDC supporters broke down the radio station door, ran into the studio and left again without finding the NPP members.

---

13. The carrot and stick idea is a method of reward and punishment often used to persuade others to act in a particular way. For example, a donkey can have a carrot waved in front of it to encourage it to move in a desired direction, while simultaneously or later being beaten with a stick to also persuade it to go in the same direction.

Despite the fact that they were on the radio to debate on national politics, a comment about the chieftaincy led to vandalism and the threat of political violence. People in Tamale and Yendi told me many times that in the north you could not leave chieftaincy out of politics. Mr Ibrahim concluded the interview by saying that the ancestors were angry at this feud within the family.

The feud would never end if the Abudus could not perform the funeral rites of their regent and Mr Ibrahim was convinced that the rites would never be performed unless the NPP was back in power. This is why it was vital for the Abudus to ensure an NPP election victory. Like the Bawku chieftaincy dispute in Upper East region, the two gates view the Ghanaian state as the authority most able to legitimise or refute leadership claims in Dagbon (Lund, 2003).

Tamale and Yendi election-related violence and party politics are inextricably linked with the Dagbon chieftaincy dispute, dating back to the 1800s. Although people from both gates sometimes switch parties, and sometimes even swap gates, Mr Ibrahim and the five others I spoke with on this issue discuss the gates and their political parties interchangeably. Undoubtedly, the settling of election-related violence in the northern region cannot occur without the settling of the Dagbon chieftaincy dispute.

Ethnicity and party politics: the case of Kumasi

As Ghana's second city, the Kumasi metropolitan area had a population of 2,035,064 in 2012 (GSS, 2012). Kumasi lies in the heart of Ashanti region towards the south of the country. It is known as the primary NPP stronghold, just as Volta region is considered the main NDC stronghold (Lindberg, 2005, p.368). In the Ashanti region, the Akan are the major ethnic group. The Ashanti sub-group of the Akan was the largest in the region in 2010 with a population of 3,449,338[14].

The second-largest group in the region are the northern Mole-Dagbani with 525,742 people (GSS 2012). This is significant because just as the NPP is seen as a southern, Akan party with its stronghold in Ashanti, the Mole-Dagbani, who are northern and viewed by many Akans as NDC supporters, are in the minority. In the 2012 presidential election, NPP candidate Nana Akuffo-Addo received 70.86% of the vote in the Ashanti region, whereas the NDC's John Dramani Mahama received 28.35%. In 2008, the NPP received 72.53% of the vote and the NDC 26.01%.

These voting patterns are very common in the Ashanti region. Similar to the NPP in Northern region, as the minority political group in the Ashanti region NDC supporters are often targets of election-related violence and threats. However, unlike Northern region, party politics in Ashanti often has an ethnic

---

14. The Akan are also the most populous group in Ghana at 47% of the population. The second-largest group is the northern Mole-Dagbani who makes up 16.6%.

dimension to it, and in Kumasi where there are many northern settlers this is no less the case.

As the second city and five or six hours' drive from Tamale, Kumasi has been a major destination for many migrants from the north who are looking for better economic opportunities. A number of northern migrants settled in one of Kumasi's deprived Zongo communities[15]. The Ghanaian word *Zongo* comes from the Hausa word *Zango*, which means an area of lodging for travellers[16]. During the colonial era, the British used Zongo to describe predominantly Hausa, Islamic and stranger/settler communities in the Gold Coast[17].

In Ghana today, Zongo describes people from northern Ghana (i.e. Gonjas and Dagombas), Burkina Faso and other predominantly Muslim groups from around West Africa (such as the Hausa) who form urban communities in mostly central and southern parts of the country[18]. Although Hausa is not considered a Ghanaian language, as a West African lingua franca it also acts as the lingua franca in Zongo communities across the country.

From the early 1700s, Kumasi hosted northern Muslim traders and religious practitioners as doctors and scribes in the royal courts of the Ashanti kingdom. This group of Muslims was eventually absorbed into the Ashanti ethnic group. Their descendants do not view themselves as Zongos today. Northern Muslims who migrated to Kumasi during the early 1900s in the colonial era to work in the mining, farming and merchant industries first formed the Zongo communities and have remained distinct "settler" communities ever since (Schildkrout, 2006).

As communities without land, Zongos around central and southern Ghana often accuse their larger host communities (the land owners) of discrimination. Zongo people frequently migrate from the north to south and central Ghana and engage in low-paid, extremely difficult work that many host groups do not want to do. One of the most notorious jobs is as a kayayei. A kayayei is often a young female porter who works in a large market, carrying heavy loads on her head for a shop trader from one part of the market to another.

This work is extremely laborious and very poorly paid. An Ashanti man and Kumasi resident said that people may call out "animal" to a kayayei as she walks past, because the task of carrying huge loads on one's body is a task associated with beasts of burden. Zongo people therefore often have low status and in

---

15. Accra is approximately 12 hours from Tamale and even further from Upper West and Upper East regions. Therefore, northerners may make up a significantly large group in greater Accra, but they are most populous in the Ashanti region and its capital Kumasi.

16. For the purposes of this study, I use the Ghanaian spelling Zongo.

17. The Gold Coast was the colonial name for what would become Ghana at independence in 1957.

18. Although Zongo communities exist in northern Ghana, they are not usually composed of northern Ghanaians but "settler" Hausa and Mossi groups from Burkina Faso.

Kumasi, which is an NPP stronghold, the Zongo are usually regarded as NDC supporters because they are northerners. This sometimes leads to conflict at election time.

Many of the perceived settler groups such as the Hausa have been in Ghana since the late 1800s, yet are still considered foreigners by many Ghanaians and the State (Schildkrout, 2006). Zongo areas are often economically deprived with high levels of unemployment, illiteracy and low-paid work. These are the factors that many informants state for why young men from Zongo areas are willing to resort to internal community violence on a day-to-day basis as well as external community violence during election time for gains.

Interviewees frequently said that "Zongo boys" and northerners in general "don't fear anything" and would be more willing to go further in undertaking all sorts of tasks for financial, social and political gains. Zongo communities are seen as "rough" areas and the various northern conflicts are frequently cited as examples of the "violent" nature of northerners. Thus Zongo and urban northern Ghanaian cities such as Tamale are places where political leaders at the local and national levels (who are commonly southerners) recruit security personnel and macho men to disrupt elections.

Notwithstanding their popular association with violence, the two Zongo community members I interviewed considered their communities as close-knit, with people who try to help one another (particularly in the face of discrimination from host community members). Although some Zongo ethnic groups are viewed as indigenous Ghanaians (such as the Dagomba or Gonja), they nonetheless have a strong imagined community (Anderson, 2006), which comprises a shared history based on Islam, migration from the north and border areas of Ghana and mutual comprehension of the Hausa language.

Moreover, a Christian, ethnically Ewe interviewee who was originally from the eastern Volta region said that Zongo communities are also very accepting of others from different ethnic groups and religions. He had grown up in a Zongo community in Kumasi and considered himself to be – and felt accepted by his community as – a Zongo, particularly because he spoke Hausa. This close tie to one's community, as well as the necessity of anonymity means that macho men are rarely recruited to disrupt the electoral process within their own communities. They are more likely to be sent to different locations around the country to do this. For example, a macho man from Kumasi's Aboabo Zongo area in the Ashanti region may be sent to Eastern region or another part of Kumasi to disrupt the polls there.

Macho men exist in the imagined national history (Anderson, 2006) of Ghanaian election-related violence as thugs, who political leaders commonly hire during elections to snatch ballot boxes and intimidate voters at polling stations in various places around the country. In Ghana, the term macho man can be used to describe any man who enjoys working out and body-building, but those who are typically involved in electoral violence and intimidation are young men from deprived Zongo communities and northern ethnic groups. Men from economically deprived areas frequently body-build to find work as security or land guards.

Macho men were originally thought of as private, unofficial land guards before they were associated with the political arena[19]. Every interviewee I discussed macho men with said that what makes the Zongo/northern areas of Ghana a favoured site to recruit macho men is the belief that men from these areas are more willing to go further and take more risks than men from outside these communities. My interviewees in Tamale, Kumasi, Accra and from Zongos all expressed the perception of physically big Zongo/northern men being hired as political thugs during elections.

Since the 2012 election, a group of bodybuilders have been trying to change their image from political thugs to concerned citizenry (Utas, 2012b) in Ghana's public domain. In January 2012, Nana Kwabena Boakye created an association called Macho Men for Good and Justice (MMGJ). With headquarters in Kumasi and a membership base of more than 6,000 people around the country, the association's objective is to tackle issues related to the welfare of macho men and Ghana as a whole.

The group aims to discourage macho men from allowing themselves to be used by politicians and to encourage them to be involved in positive tasks for the nation instead. For example, the association advocates for more employment opportunities for young body-builders, including the suggestion that they could be partnered with official security task forces during elections to guard ballot boxes. Alternatively, they could be involved in the small-scale mining or agricultural sectors. In a forum that Graphic Communications Ltd organised, Boakye stated that the cost to the lives and welfare of young macho men rarely significantly outweighed the gains. This has particularly been the case when politicians have dropped macho men once they have won power and refused to

---

19. A land guard is typically a physically stocky man hired by landowners as informal bailiffs to force squatters off of landowners' land.

pay them for completed work (Ghana News Agency, 2012)[20]. Gainful employment could play a role in diverting macho men from working for politicians and against the democratic process during elections.

The MMGJ, which has assisted young men in finding work and helping with security during the 2012 elections, is trying to change the public image of bodybuilders as trouble makers in Ghana. The case of macho men from deprived areas trying to involve themselves in elections in a positive way is a public example of the struggle that can ensue in new democracies where concerned citizens have conflicting loyalties to big men and the nation (Utas, 2012b).

Narratives of Kumasi elections

In Kumasi I interviewed a man called Alex in his early twenties who had grown up in a Zongo community there and recently moved from the area. Alex's boss, Kwame, who is Ashanti and an NPP supporter, introduced me to him. Kwame also sat with us at the interview and contributed to the discussion from time to time. Alex classed himself as Ewe (originally from the Volta region), however, he strongly identified with the northerners he grew up with in the Zongo community and could speak Hausa, the Zongo lingua franca.

Alex was an NDC supporter but was cynical about politicians in general, saying that "they are all the same". He did not vote in 2012 because he had travelled away from where he was registered. He had not heard about or seen any violence. Our conversation then turned to macho men and the Zongo community.

> CA: *"Do you know anything about these macho men? Do you know where they are coming from most of the time?"*
>
> Alex: *"You know in this country there is some people they call land guards… They used to lift metals [weights] and build their bodies for such work."*
>
> CA: *"Are they official in anyway?"*
>
> Alex: *"No. They are the same people that, when it gets to election time, people go and hire them and take ballot boxes where they feel they cannot win. They lift weights for work. If they lift weights and they are big you fear them, so macho men…It is only this election that they formed a group and they came out that they are going to protect the election… You see their symbols on their cars."*
>
> Kwame: *"My friend you saw, the NPP came at a particular time and asked him to be a macho man, a body guard. A member who associates with the MP came and*

20. In 2012, the winner of TV3's body-building competition *Ghana's Strongest Man,* Faisal Alhassan, also spoke about his desire to work with young macho men. Alhassan, who is from the city of Wa in Upper West region (one of the two northern regions bordering Burkina Faso) said that he wanted to educate youths, and especially macho men, to refrain from allowing politicians to use them in elections. He launched his "Operation Violent Free 2012 Elections" [sic] in Wa in 2012 (Alhassan, 2011).

asked him to work as a macho man. If you can help them when they win you can become their security."

Earlier that afternoon when walking with Kwame, he had come across a tall, stocky friend of his whom he had greeted in the street. This example reflects how tall, stocky men can be randomly approached by a party member with links to an MP. However, this kind of random selection of macho men is not always how MPs recruit[21].

CA: *"Where can you find macho men?"*

Alex: *"You can find them through gym; you can find them through someone who knows them. Maybe If I know one macho man and you come and see me that, Chale[22], I want you and your guys to do so sososo[23] for me. Because we fear the body-builders so far as they have been put in the place that they should protect that place, you will not even go there."*

CA: *"What is the social background of many macho men? Where are they often coming from?"*

Alex: *"I would say a lot of them are coming from the [Zongo] community… It's from infancy we know that they are the people who do not fear anything. It's been made to an extent that we believe it and they have proven us right, too…There are places that you will send me I would not go, the Zongo guy he would go."*

Given that Zongo communities were predominantly northern and vote NDC, I was interested to know if most macho men – who are often recruited from these areas – would be willing to work for the NPP.

CA: *"Can an NPP person go and say 'Come and be my macho man'?"*

Alex: *"They will go, even if the person is a strong NDC member. If he does not get what he wants from NDC, from people from NDC camp, he will go. One interesting thing is that, when you get to the Zongo community, the NDC are more. You'll find NPP too but they will not fight."*

Kwame: *"No they will not fight, but if they want to fight they'll bring another from another Zongo community…They go outside and do that [fight], they do not do it within their own community."*

Kwame here highlights the tactics of politicians recruiting macho men from a particular area and sending them to a polling station in another town or part of the country to cause havoc. Alex pointed out that most macho men are Muslims "and you know so far as they are Muslims they form themselves as one". Thus,

---

21. See Appendix 1 for an example of how an "honourable" recruits a macho man.
22. *Chale* is Ghanaian slang that can be translated as "mate" or "man" in English
23. Sososo Can be translated as do "different things" or do "this, this and this"

though Macho men may go to different areas to cause problems, they are loyal to their own particular communities.

> CA: *"Which politicians or party leaders go and get these macho men?"*
>
> Kwame: *"It can be anybody, but actually they always depend on local people like us because once they have names, they have positions, so they will often consult people like us."*

Earlier that day in Kumasi I had also interviewed the NPP co-ordinator for the Subin constituency in Kumasi central, Mr Yeboah, who had spoken about the activities of macho men during elections. Mr Yeboah is an Ashanti man in his fifties. He had observed a calm election in 2012. Of the four interviewees I asked about why they felt elections were largely peaceful that year, I was usually given a reason why it had not been peaceful in previous years, rather than why it was peaceful in 2012. Peace seemed to be something that was expected.

According to Mr Yeboah, the reason for the 2012 peace was that there was no tense run-off and people did not want a similar level of tension to 2008 and 2004. The biometric voting system also made it pointless for people to try to register and vote multiple times, leading to one reason why less violent incidences occurred. During the 2004 and 2008 elections, Mr Yeboah's area of Subin experienced cases of ballot box-snatching by macho men on motorcycles.

According to Mr Yeboah, in one case, a macho man had started an argument with a voter at the polling station and slapped that person for no reason, making everybody turn their attention to the commotion. A second macho man then rode past on a motorbike[24] and snatched a ballot box. That particular polling station only had one police officer guarding it who was outnumbered by macho men. The result of this kind of situation is that potential voters may become scared over the events at the polling station, leave the queue and not return to vote.

Mr Yeboah said that this kind of scenario typically happened in strongholds where one of the two large parties did not feel it could win. They would consequently engineer a plan to snatch a ballot box to have the polling station voided

---

24. Motorbikes have a strong negative association with political violence and disruption in Ghana, because a rider can rapidly go to a location, cause mayhem and easily get away. Cars are the most common method of transport in the south, whereas motorbikes are more frequently used in the north. Young men on motorbikes causing trouble is a common image described by interviewees. Men on motorbikes were said to snatch ballot boxes at polling stations, ride through towns and have occasional confrontations in the street with one another when they were working for political parties. This image of menacing men on motorbikes has taken on such serious dimensions that in the northern town of Bawku, where conflict has endured for more than 50 years (Aganah, 2008), men have been banned from riding motorbikes. A Bawku student of mine said that if a person visits Bawku now, where few people own non-commercial vehicles, they would see only women on motorbikes and men mostly on bicycles (Daily Guide, 2010).

or the ballot box tampered with. Another incident that occurred in Subin happened while Mr Yeboah was counting ballot papers at the St Paul's school in a crowd of people. Stones were thrown into the crowd and one hit Mr Yeboah on the head. The polling station was in a mixed area, however, the NPP had a slight majority.

Although it faces similar problems with macho men as in many parts of the country, as an Ashanti stronghold Kumasi's political environment has an ethnic colouring that seems more pronounced than in Accra. The following case clearly illustrates the ethnic dimensions of politics in the Ashanti region. Joe is a student at the Kwame Nkrumah University of Science and Technology (KNUST) in Kumasi, the nation's foremost university that specialises in the sciences.

Joe is studying agricultural science and is in his final year of an undergraduate degree. He grew up outside Kumasi and has lived in Kumasi as a student for four years. He did not have time to meet me while I was in Kumasi, but agreed to a telephone interview instead. He became a card-carrying NDC party member six months ago and now says that his "heart is for the party."

Joe stated that earlier in his life, he had not been interested in being active in politics. His mother was an NDC supporter and his father an NPP man. He grew up in the Ashanti homeland as an Ashanti and always preferred the NPP, like his father's family. Joe said that he had been brought up like a "typical Ashanti", always thinking that his ethnic group was the best and that northerners were bad people who were always involved in "fetishism and other ungodly, wicked things".

Joe explained that people often split up and grouped themselves together by region at KNUST. Even when group assignments were given during class, Ashantis usually wanted to work together, and northerners also worked together. As a minority group in a southern majority university, northern students consequently started social groups, such as a Muslim and northern association to "encourage themselves". With time, Joe started to become friends with some northerners and realised that they were not all bad.

Following a violent encounter with the NPP one day, Joe eventually decided to switch from the NPP and become an NDC supporter. During the heated 2008 elections, Joe had voted for the NPP in the first round. Before the country went to the run-off round, soldiers visited his house. The soldiers said that they had had a tip-off from somebody that Joe's grandfather had sent macho men to stay at Joe's house and that they were there to snatch ballot boxes during the election run-off. Even though Joe's father was a known NPP supporter, his NDC mother's side of the family had raised the authorities' suspicions.

Joe's maternal grandfather is a relative of the mother of former NDC president Jerry John Rawlings (1993–2001) and had previously held a ministerial position in the Rawlings government. The soldiers proceeded to ransack Joe's house, looking for macho men, and slapped Joe in the face. Joe said that he had always been taught that northerners were violent "but the slap I received showed how the NPP could be violent."

After this incident in 2008, Joe decided to start supporting the NDC. This was not because he felt that the NDC was necessarily a better party than the NPP; in fact, Joe had felt that they were both as bad as one another and neither would make major improvements to Ghana. Yet with his grandfather's contacts, and since people assumed that he was an NDC member anyway, Joe reasoned that he may as well join the NDC and try to personally benefit from them through his grandfather.

Joe also spoke of violent incidents he had heard about in Kumasi after elections. A small crowd of NDC supporters were celebrating in a street in Kumasi the day after the elections. An NPP supporter who was driving a car told them to get off the road or he would run them over. They did not stop and the driver knocked three people over. One person died and two were sent to hospital but recovered. Joe said that the man is now in prison.

An NDC shop assistant was sacked by her NPP employer after she was found celebrating the NDC win at work. An NDC woman told Joe that her NPP *susu* colleagues would no longer allow her to take part in their susu because the NDC had won the elections fraudulently. Currently the NPP is taking the electoral commission and the NDC to court on charges of electoral fraud. There is a general feeling among NPP supporters that they have been cheated out of the presidency.

Despite all of these reported incidents, Joe was generally happy with how the elections went and felt that they had been very peaceful and much better than in 2008. He said that the biometric voting system was the main thing that had made things smoother and stopped the parties from ballot stuffing.

The case of Greater Accra
Greater Accra's population totalled 4,010,054 in 2010 (GSS, 2012). At the generally peaceful 2012 election, much of the politically motivated violence in Ghana happened in Accra. The democratic credentials of the NDC and the police were called into question when police in full riot gear raided an NPP office in central Accra on 10th December 2012. A group of NPP supporters had been conducting forensic audits of the elections. The NPP was gathering evidence for a court case it was bringing against President John Dramani Mahama for electoral fraud.

On 12 December, the police issued a statement that they had searched the NPP office because they had received a tip-off that a group of macho men were storing weapons in a house. The NPP claimed that the police had taken important documents and laptops away with them, but the police said that they had not taken anything away (Myjoyonline.com, 2012). The NPP maintained that this incident had been a government ploy to try to intimidate NPP members and take important data and files that the NPP would use to build a court case against Mahama. This story was discussed in the media for a few days before it died down. The media are now following the court case between the NDC and the NPP.

The day before the police search, a man wearing an NDC t-shirt was stabbed during an NPP post-election demonstration at Kwame Nkrumah Circle. Demonstrators were protesting about the election results, which had been announced on 9 December confirming that Mahama had won the presidency. The actual events leading up to the stabbing are not known (Gadugah, 2012).

John Arday was among the demonstrators. John is an NPP coordinator of "party foot soldiers" as he calls them. In interview he said that he had not seen the stabbing and thought it may not even have been an NDC man that was stabbed. He said that there was no evidence that the man was wearing an NDC t-shirt and that it was probably just an NDC ploy to make the NPP look as violent as the NDC were.

John is a strong NPP supporter and was eager to discuss the work of coordinators. According to John, "foot soldiers" is the term big men use to denote the rank and file supporters of their parties. John believed that foot soldiers were the "strong-bone" and the "roots" because they make up the majority in a party. Foot soldiers typically make up the mass of supporters at party rallies and public demonstrations. This rank and file usually consists of less-educated men, in the main, who are unemployed or work in low-paid occupations such as masonry, carpentry and taxi driving.

John usually coordinates this group of people. He said that a foot soldier coordinator could be a person who has gained the trust and friendship of an MP or other party big man. The coordinator may help the MP in many different ways, from fixing things around the house to doing odd jobs for him. John himself got to know a top-ranking NPP politician (he would not say who) through an elderly friend of his. With this introduction, John began doing odd jobs and running errands for the politician.

John came to know the big man well and became a trusted ally. Once the politician knew that John had links to many people in town, such as the unemployed, taxi drivers, masons and so on he became the politician's main coordinator, particularly of young men in the area. John said that coordinators are not always illiterate; they may have a senior high school education, but that is usually their highest qualification.

Coordinators bring people together for rallies, demonstrations and meetings via word-of-mouth and receive political largesse to distribute among the foot soldiers. Coordinators may themselves occasionally help foot soldiers when they are financially constrained. If their party comes into power, coordinators may also help foot soldiers into public jobs such as the police and fire services, which require little educational qualifications to enter.

MPs and top politicians sometimes give money to coordinators and foot soldiers to call into radio talk shows to defend the party. MPs at times forge direct links with a few foot soldiers in their constituency by paying their children's school fees, for example. This makes those receiving the money loyally defend the MP, whether the MP is in the right or wrong, since their own welfare depends on the MP's success.

Nevertheless, John wanted me to know that foot soldiers do not necessarily need to be given money to gain their loyalty. He made it clear that an MP simply could not pay everybody and the scraps of largesse a common foot soldier received would rarely amount to much. John explained that if foot soldiers saw that an MP was really working towards providing even one important facility to the community (e.g. electricity, a school, a hospital) then they would remember this for many years to come.

Wherever they go, high-ranking politicians may have different coordinators to do things for them, such as provide security for the venue they may speak at and mobilise people for them to give speeches to audiences. However, it is not always easy for MPs to control coordinators and foot soldiers, and they do not always get what they want from them. If MPs are not generous enough in distributing money among constituents or do nothing to improve or visit their constituency, foot soldiers and coordinators may back their own independent candidate to stand against the MP.

Demonstrations such as the ones that took place in Accra and Kumasi were partly organised by coordinators such as John. John said that violence at these mass gatherings is often unorganised (meaning that they happened spontaneously), were difficult to control and strongly depend on the attitude of the foot soldiers as to whether or not a demonstration stays peaceful.

Instability in employment: the civil service and business people in Accra

It is not only the poorest groups in Ghana who stake their livelihoods on political outcomes. The risk of losing work is high among the middle classes who are employed in the public and private sectors if somebody's favoured party does not come to power. Regina is from an upper-middle class background. She told me about the experiences of her father and her mother's friend, who were both civil servants working in top managerial positions and knew that retaining their jobs depended on politics.

When the NDC regained power in 2008, Regina's father was given the position of director in one of the largest civil service departments in the country. If the NDC lost in 2012, Regina and her family were scared that her father would lose his job. Regina's father told her that if you gained a civil service position through politics, then you would most likely be replaced if another political party gained power.

Those who worked their way up through the ranks could often remain in high managerial positions, though they would have fierce competition from externally recruited employees such as Regina's father. This is because those who had helped the party with financial contributions to its campaigns needed to be reimbursed through highly paid jobs. The political sacking of civil servants became very high profile when in 2000 the NPP under John Kufuor won the presidency following 19 years under Rawlings.

The friend of Regina's mother worked in the Ministry of Finance at the time and lost her job soon after. Regina explained:

> *"They maintained their civil servants in their position until sensitive information leaked out about the budget…They sacked people who had access to the information who were not loyal or an NPP… They were competent, that's why they maintained them, but the leaking of information was the problem."*

The NPP saw the leaking of information as a deliberate political act of sabotage by NDC supporters who had been working under the NDC government for many years. The NPP replaced many workers with civil servants who were sympathetic to the party. Here, national politics not only affected workers in high-ranking positions, but also those working in secretarial positions. Although the sacking of lower-ranking civil servants is rare, special circumstances such as this can arise and threaten them too.

Fortunately for Regina's mother's friend, when the NDC regained the presidency in 2008, she was able to find government-related work again: her employer got a contract from the NDC and asked her to work with him on it. In common with presidential/parliamentary work, the high level of instability within the civil service at the top ranks means that many people working in this sector want to take their slice of the national cake while they can, before the party loses power (Bayart, 1993), particularly when they have debts to repay from election campaigns.

The civil service is not the only sector at risk when the government changes hands. John Osei is a wealthy businessman who works in the shipping sector in Tema, Greater Accra, and has sometimes lost business because of politics. Despite the fact that he has a preferred party, he claims that like many other business people, he tries to stay out of politics because you could lose your business as soon as a party you do not belong to comes to power. Mr Osei also felt that the NPP started "polarisation" during their eight-year rule when they took over from Rawlings and the NDC. Mr Osei had initially voted for the NPP to get into power because he had wanted a change from NDC rule, but later regretted his decision:

"Nationalists like us decided that it was time for NPP also to come... I'm a victim of it, myself sitting down here. When they don't see you in their party papers, you don't belong to them, you are NDC so they should spoil your business. Let's assume like me... In Tema oil refinery, I was their biggest supplier. I supplied them most of their things and everything... Their pipings, materials. Everything I supplied them. I was one of their biggest suppliers. The record is there. They thought I was an NDC and blacklisted me!"

When workers at the oil refinery were unable to find the materials they needed with their preferred suppliers, they went to buy them from Mr Osei. During one visit to Mr Osei the buyers from the oil refinery told him that he had been blacklisted by their superiors and they felt it was unfair that their management was doing this to him. Mr Osei believes that the NPP started the kind of nepotism in Ghana wherein people lost jobs and business with the change of government: "When Rawlings was removed out of power, or let's say NDC was removed out of power, this is what they brought in! Polarisation! This is what [happened] from 2000 to 2008!"

When job insecurity increases during elections, people have a greater stake in ensuring that their party wins at all costs. This can affect the democratic process, because the middle classes can also be in positions of responsibility during elections: they can act as election observers and in counting rooms, for example. When someone's livelihood depends on the outcome of elections, ensuring that the election process is free and fair may sometimes come into conflict with one's immediate need to remain employed and provide for one's family.

Concluding remarks

I have studied election-related violence in three different regions in Ghana (Greater Accra, Yendi/Tamale and Kumasi) to try to explore the dynamics and possible causes of violence during elections in the country.

Causes of violence

Despite the similarities between the three selected localities when it comes to election-related violence, there are also important differences. In Yendi/Tamale, chieftaincy cannot be separated from elections and election-related violence. The most severe violence took place in Yendi, where the Ya-Naa of Dagbon was killed in 2002. Whether or not the NPP government was involved on the side of the Abudus as the Andani gate asserts, the claim that the NPP/Abudu alignment led to the death of the Ya-Naa Andani has led to fierce political rivalry between the two gates.

This rivalry has often been expressed during election periods. As Mr Ibrahim and an Andani interviewee said, the conflict in the north cannot be resolved if the chieftaincy dispute is left unresolved. If gates continue to be tied to particular political parties in exchange for votes and general political support, it is difficult to imagine how the cycle of intra-ethnic violence during elections in Dagbon could come to an end. The solution may perhaps lie in a more locally based reconciliation effort.

In contrast to the Northern region's intra-ethnic conflict, Kumasi's politics hints at very strong divisions between ethnic groups. Ethnicity and politics is more pronounced than in the north; the NPP is seen as an ethnic-Ashanti party and the NDC as a northern/Ewe party. The voting patterns in the Ashanti and Volta regions have confirmed these regions as solid strongholds of the NPP and NDC respectively. Violence and tensions have seemingly often erupted when the minority NDC supporters openly celebrated an NDC win. Violence usually comes in the form of intimidation of minority supporters by an NPP majority.

In Accra, no interviewee discussed ethnicity unless it was in a very general way and with reference to the country as a whole. Ethnicity and electoral violence, however, was not related to the city at all. A violent incident between party youth wings was the most serious form of violence that the media reported in the Greater Accra region, when a man was stabbed during an NPP demonstration.

It is not only poor youths who can disrupt the democratic process. In Accra, where most of the high-ranking public sector positions and lucrative businesses are located, middle-class adults also feel at risk when the government changes hands. This causes people to understand elections as a highly risky process that could end in the loss of jobs and business. For the middle classes, elections then become something that must be won at all costs.

Perpetrators of violence

The main pattern found was that young men from northern backgrounds (whether directly from the north or Zongo communities) are frequently said to be the first choice for politicians to use to perpetrate the most violent acts during elections. Northern Ghana is often relegated to the status of a backwater: undeveloped, unimportant, wild and backward. Yet northerners have a very strong presence in the imaginations of Ghanaians when they speak of politics and violence. Zongo/northern macho men are portrayed as willing to take the risk of snatching ballot boxes and causing mayhem at polling stations.

Macho men are sent from their own areas to other locations around the country to disrupt elections. This helps these men maintain a certain level of anonymity when carrying out illegal acts. However, an organisation such as Macho Men for Good and Justice shows that since 2012 some macho men have been trying to alter their public image to present themselves as concerned citizens.

The role of big men in violence

Rarely the direct perpetrators of violence themselves, local MPs are frequently cited as a group that create space for violence. This group is mostly responsible for organised violence on Election Day and during voter registration. MPs have strong links with national political parties, party youth/youth coordinators, and local authorities. Mr Ibrahim in Tamale illustrated how MPs were very active in working between local constituents/youth, their political party and authorities such as the police to keep some of their "boys" from being charged with a crime. Local MPs are certainly crucial to organised violent conflict during elections and further research into electoral violence in Ghana should include interviews with either them or MPs currently out of power.

The most promising area to explore in further research would be the Yendi/ Tamale conflict, because of its complex links with chieftaincy, politics, kinship, urban/rural dynamics of conflict and the occurrence of election-related violence outside of election years. Though violence is always regional, the conflicts in the north seem to pose the highest security risk in the country. Because conflicts such as Yendi/Tamale are never really resolved, elections open a window for violence. Trying to further understand the Yendi/Tamale problem in relation to election-related violence offers a fruitful way to understand how Ghana can experience election-related violence but at the same time work towards the consolidation of democracy.

References

Adolfo, Eldridge, V., Söderberg Kovacs, M.,Nyström, D. and Utas, M. *Electoral Violence in Africa.* [pdf] Uppsala: Nordiska Afrikainstitutet. Available at: <http://nai.diva-portal.org/smash/get/diva2:556709/FULLTEXT01.pdf>[Accessed 8 August 2013].

Aganah, G. A. M., 2008. *The Effects of Chieftaincy Conflicts on Local Development: The Case of Bawku East Municipality.* Masters Thesis. University of Tromso.

Alhassan, I., 2011. Macho Man Campaigns Against Election Violence. The Chronicle, [Online] 25 November. Available at: http://ghanaian-chronicle.com/macho-man-campaigns-against-election-violence/ [Accessed 22 January 2013].

Anderson, B., 2006. *Imagined Communities.* London: Verso.

Bayart, J-F., 1993. *The State in Africa: The Politics of the Belly.* Essex: Longman.

Bokpe, S.J., 2012. When Machomen are Let Loose…. *Seth J. Bokpe's Ghana Newsreel.* [blog] 28 December. Available at: http://sethbnews09.blogspot.com/2012/12/when-machomen-are-let-loose.html [Accessed 22 January 2013].

Christensen, M. and Utas, M., 2008. Mercenaries of Democracy: The 'Politricks' of Remobilized Combatants in the 2007 General Elections, Sierra Leone. *African Affairs.* 107 (429), pp. 515–539.

Daily Guide, 2010. Bawku Women Free to Ride Motorbikes. *Modern Ghana* [Online] 31 May 2010. Available at: http://www.modernghana.com/news/277975/1/bawku-women-free-to-ride-motorbikes.html [Accessed 23 February 2013].

Diedong, R.D., 2012. Can There be True Peace Without Justice? Modern Ghana, [Online] 23 December. Available at: http://www.modernghana.com/news/437007/1/can-there-be-true-peace-without-justice.html [Accessed 23 February 2013].

Dirks, R., 1988. Annual Rituals of Conflict. *American Anthropologist.* 90 (4), pp. 856–870.

Drucker-Brown, S., 1999. The Grandchildren's Play at the Mamprusi King's Funeral: Ritual Rebellion Revisted in Northern Ghana. *The Journal of the Royal Anthropological Institute.* 5 (2), pp.181–192.

Freiku, S.R., 2012. Macho Men Want to Monitor Election 2012… To Protect Lives, Property. *The Chronicle*, [Online] 18 October. Available at: <http://ghanaian-chronicle.com/macho-men-want-to-monitor-election-2012-to-protect-lives-property/> [Accessed 22 January 2013].

Gadugah, N., 2012. NDC Man Stabbed by Irate NPP Supporters. *Myjoyonline.com.* [Online] 11 December. Available at <http://edition.myjoyonline.com/pages/news/201212/98539.php> [Accessed 22 January 2013].

Ghana News Agency, 2012. Youth Must Shun Political Violence – 'Machomen Group'. *Ghana News Agency*, [Online] 3 December 2012. Available at ,http://ghananewsagency.org/politics/youth-must-shun-political-violence-machomen-group-53251. [Accessed 26 January 2013].

Ghana Statistical Service, 2012. 2010 *Population and Housing Census: Summary Report of Final Results,* [Online] Accra: Ghana Statistical Service. Available at <http://www.statsghana.gov.gh/docfiles/2010phc/Census2010_Summary_report_of_final_results.pdf> [Accessed 20 January 2013].

Hennemeyer, C.R., 2011. Democracy in Africa: Rumours of its Demise is Greatly Exaggerated in: D. Gillies, ed. 2011. *Elections in Dangerous Places: Democracy and the Paradoxes of Peacebuilding.* Montreal: McGill-Queen's University Press.

Hughes, T., 2003. *Managing Group Grievances and Conflict: Ghana Country Report.* Netherlands Institute of International Relations Working Paper 11, The Hague.

Ibrahim, U., 2012. *Interview on Elections in Ghana.* Tamale Central. Interview by Clementina Amankwaah. 2 January 2013.

Jockers, H.,Kohnert, D. and Nugent, P., 2009. *The Successful Ghana Election of 2008: A Convenient Myth? Ethnicity in Ghana's Election Revisited* [pdf] Available at <http://mpra.ub.uni-muenchen.de/16167/1/MPRA_paper_16167.pdf> [Accessed 27 January 2013].

Lindberg. S and Morrison. M., 2005. Exploring Voter Alignments in Africa: Core and Swing Voters in Ghana. *Journal of Modern African Studies.* 43(4), pp. 565–586.

Lindberg. S and Morrison. M., 2008. Are African Voters Really Ethnic or Clientilistic? Survey Evidence from Ghana. *Political Science Quarterly.* 123 (1), pp. 95–122.

Lund, C., 2003. Bawku is still Volatile: Ethno-Politico Conflict and State Recognition in Northern Ghana. *Journal of Modern Africa Studies.* [e-journal]. 41 (4). Abstract Only. Available at <http://www.jstor.org/discover/10.2307/3876355?imd=3738072&imd=2&imd=4&sid=21101610002011> [Accessed on 22 January 2013].

Mansfield, E.D and Snyder, J. 2007. *Electing to Fight: Why Emerging Democracies go to War.* MIT Press: Cambridge.

Myjoyonline.com, 2012. Police deny raiding NPP office; Bediatuo insists they did. *Myjoyonline.com,*[Online] 11 December. Available at <http://politics.myjoyonline.com/pages/news/201212/98561.php> [Accessed on 23 January 2013]

National Electoral Commission, 2012. [Online], Available at <http://www.ec.gov.gh/index.php> [Accessed on 2 March 2013].

Schildkrout, E., 2006. Chieftaincy and Emerging Identities: Establishing legitimacy in immigrant communities in Ghana and the Diaspora. In: I. K. Odotei and A. K. Awedoba, eds. 2006. *Chieftaincy in Ghana: Culture, Governance and Development.* Accra: Sub Saharan Publishers, pp. 587–601.

United Nations Cartographic Section (2005) *Ghana* [Online]. Available at: http://www.un.org/Depts/Cartographic/english/htmain.htm [Accessed January 27]

Utas, M., 2012a. Introduction: Bigmanity and Network Governance in African Conflicts. In: M. Utas, ed. 2012, *African Conflicts and Informal Power: Big Men and Networks.* London: Zed Books, pp. 1–31.

Utas, M., 2012b. *Discussion about Ghana's Relevance to Research on Elections and Violence in New Democracies.* [Conversation] (Personal Communication 5 December 2012)

Weiss, H., 2005. *Contested Historical and Geographic Narratives: SuccessionDisputes, Contested Land Ownership and Religious Conflicts in Northern Ghana.* Abo Akademi and University of Helsinki Working Papers on Ghana: Historical and Contemporary Studies Number 6.

Appendix 1

The short story and commentary below has been taken from a newsreel blog post by a journalist, Seth Bokpe (2012). I attempted to get the story directly from the source stated in the post, *The Daily Graphic newspaper,* but to no avail. However, I have included the post because it gives a detailed depiction of the experiences of macho men during elections and could be a very insightful peace once the credibility and origin of the source has been identified.

When Machomen are Let Loose...

It is a hot afternoon on December 7, 2004. The sticky hot air notwithstanding, long queue of voters snake across the dusty school park, anxiety written over their faces.

Not far away, Mad Lion, the leader of the muscled men, sits restlessly on the edge of the concrete pillar holding up the wooden bridge. He chuckles to himself with satisfaction as he monitors the rowdy behaviour of the group he calls "The Boys".

Occasionally, they would stop a voter suspected to likely cast the ballot for the party they are opposed to. Angered or intimidated, the potential voter would turn around and head home. The few brave ones who dared to ask questions get away with a bloodied mouth or a twisted arm.

Mad Lion would occasionally intervene but not without advising the victim to vote for 'honourable,' his preferred candidate.

That is not all, electoral officers are occasionally forced to allow some voters to jump the queue. With shirts off and their bulging muscles on display, the strictest presiding officer snaps to attention to carry out the order.

The night before, Mad Lion had met 'honourable' behind the scenes to sort out what is due 'The Boys'. The election was down to the wire and "honourable's" image has seen a downward trend since the last election. His sense of optimism has developed wings.

"Listen, this race is stiff; I want you to concentrate on the list I have given you. Go to those polling stations and muddy the waters as much as you can. If possible snatch one or two ballot boxes before the counting begins."

"There will be a team waiting for you right under the overpass, swap the contents of the box and later abandon it where they can easily see it."

"Lion, remember no mistakes. I will try as much as possible to cover you guys, but if you make any grievous mistakes, you are on your own. Here is half of the cash I promised," "honourable" said wiping the film of sweat dripping down his brow.

Mad Lion pulls out the wad of cash from the polythene bag, sniffs it with some air of satisfaction, he drops the cash back into his pocket and put up a pensive face.

With the cash in his pocket, he looks honourable in the face and stammers, "ho-ho-honourable, this one is baaack pay for fu-fu-four yeeeears ago. After the job, we no see you again. If you no pay for this year, we no go do the job."

Honourable shocked at the turn of events punched his right palm with a clenched left fist. He removes his cap, pulls out his handkerchief and mops his face. Then, a willy[sic] grin crosses his face before he spoke, "Lion listen, I will do you guys fine, I promise. Four years ago, I spent so much the pocket dried after the elections. Listen I will take care of you later and I mean it. You know me."

To that, Mad Lion shakes his head and mumbles, "Honourable, you said that in 1996 and all those boys think say, I collect the money den chop. You no see seyibi different boys I dey use now?"

With a defeated demeanour, the MP dips his hand into his pocket and strikes Lion on the chest with wads of cash that scatters on the floor. Casting his eyes around, as if his location was a forbidden one, he walked out of the uncompleted gym full of car rims disgimsed [sic] as weightlifting equipment.

That night lubricated with a few bottles of beer, The Boys planned their strategy to intimidate and cause chaos at not less [sic] 10 polling stations.

Just about 20 minutes' walk from Mad Lion's meeting base, another group of lawless boys are planning a similar campaign with honourable's main opponent.

Back to the polling station, Roberta Kekeli, a Polling Assistant, is checking names of voters with fear determining every step. "I am frightened because trouble is not far away," she said looking around at the rowdy squad of muscled youth.

The polling station had been promised a security person, but by mid-afternoon none of Accra's finest had bothered to show up.

Trouble's ugly head appeared when two young men walked to the polling station, jumped the queue, voted but refused to leave the station.

At that moment, Mad Lion nodded to a tall heavily-bearded young man in shorts. The rascal walked quietly over to the Presidential ballot box, picked it and jumped onto a motorbike and disappeared.

Another person dashed to the parliamentary ballot box but met resistance from one of the three young men. A melee ensued between The Boys and young men who by now have increased in numbers. The struggle over the ballot boxes continued as if their very lives depended on it.

With everyone pushing and shoving but never crossing that fine line into full-fledge [sic] brawl, the electoral officials stared in disbelieve[sic]. Half-hearted voters chorused "no macho men," but this vaporised as soon as Mad Lion jumped from his sitting position, chest out and with calculated heavy steps began to move close to the commotion.

Just when all hope of avoiding [sic] punch-up was vanishing in the hot afternoon air, a van pulled up and emptied a dozen policemen.

As if with[sic] on cue, the shouting immediately died, the macho men dispersed, and the voters snapped into a disciplined line.

A bulky-looking officer screamed at his men to take position. A few minutes later, total order was restored and voting business continued with Roberta and his colleagues now at ease.

The policemen pranced around for a few minutes before returning to their vehicles in preparation to depart.

"The scenario above is not far from real as it is a real life story shared with The Daily Graphic by a Macho man who only asked to be called Mad Lion."

"[25]At the centre of the reported cases of violence and intimidation, which is burning the country's electoral integrity at the stake, are allegations of well-bimlt[sic] or muscled young men popularly referred to as 'Machos' in Ghana parading electoral areas during elections for reasons best known to particularly the two strongest political parties–the National Democratic Congress and the New Patriotic Party."

These thugs sprung from relative obscurity and became part of the country's political sphere at the dawn of the Fourth Republic. The phenomenon has become so engraved in the country's electoral culture that, during the 2004, 2008 and subsequent by-elections, macho men became endangered species, with callers to radio phone-in programmes openly declaring that they would organise to 'deal' with any macho man seen around polling stations.

The NDC and the NPP were also at each other's throat for engaging the 'muscle-men' during the 2008 general election and by-elections held afterward with the current MP for Assin North, Mr. Kennedy Agyepong, alleged to have openly said he engaged a thousand muscled men in 2008 to protect the interest of the party.

Supporters of the parties in attempts to rationalise the engagement of these characters have linked it to attempts by the two parties to increase their presence on the ground to protect the ballots, but the result has always been chaos.

25. This bolded section is the comments of the blogger, Seth Bokpe, on Mad Lion's story.

It is in the light of these that the decision of Machomen for Good and Justice, an association of body builders, to adopt a stance against violence and intimidation in the electoral process should be applauded.

From their own gruelling accounts, many of their colleagues from 1992 have either been killed or maimed. But their paymasters always avoid them right after the elections.

While it will be difficult to control all these people, the commitment of a few to ensuring that the election is free of intimidation would breathe more air of confidence into the process.

Nana Osei, a member of the association, aptly summarised what many of us feel about Macho men who channel their energy into nothing but elections, 'I am saddened when people say Ghanaian Macho men are stealing ballot boxes when their colleagues elsewhere are winning Olympic medals.'"

CURRENT AFRICAN ISSUES PUBLISHED BY THE INSTITUTE

Recent issues in the series are available electronically
for download free of charge www.nai.uu.se

1981

1. *South Africa, the West and the Frontline States. Report from a Seminar.*

2. Maja Naur, *Social and Organisational Change in Libya.*

3. *Peasants and Agricultural Production in Africa. A Nordic Research Seminar. Follow-up Reports and Discussions.*

1985

4. Ray Bush & S. Kibble, *Destabilisation in Southern Africa, an Overview.*

5. Bertil Egerö, *Mozambique and the Southern African Struggle for Liberation.*

1986

6. Carol B.Thompson, *Regional Economic Polic under Crisis Condition. Southern African Development.*

1989

7. Inge Tvedten, *The War in Angola, Internal Conditions for Peace and Recovery.*

8. Patrick Wilmot, *Nigeria's Southern Africa Policy 1960–1988.*

1990

9. Jonathan Baker, *Perestroika for Ethiopia: In Search of the End of the Rainbow?*

10. Horace Campbell, *The Siege of Cuito Cuanavale.*

1991

11. Maria Bongartz, *The Civil War in Somalia. Its genesis and dynamics.*

12. Shadrack B.O. Gutto, *Human and People's Rights in Africa. Myths, Realities and Prospects.*

13. Said Chikhi, Algeria. *From Mass Rebellion to Workers' Protest.*

14. Bertil Odén, *Namibia's Economic Links to South Africa.*

1992

15. Cervenka Zdenek, *African National Congress Meets Eastern Europe. A Dialogue on Common Experiences.*

1993

16. Diallo Garba, *Mauritania–The Other Apartheid?*

1994

17. Zdenek Cervenka and Colin Legum, *Can National Dialogue Break the Power of Terror in Burundi?*

18. Erik Nordberg and Uno Winblad, *Urban Environmental Health and Hygiene in Sub-Saharan Africa.*

1996

19. Chris Dunton and Mai Palmberg, *Human Rights and Homosexuality in Southern Africa.*

1998

20. Georges Nzongola-Ntalaja, *From Zaire to the Democratic Republic of the Congo.*

1999

21. Filip Reyntjens, *Talking or Fighting? Political Evolution in Rwanda and Burundi, 1998–1999.*

22. Herbert Weiss, *War and Peace in the Democratic Republic of the Congo.*

2000

23. Filip Reyntjens, *Small States in an Unstable Region – Rwanda and Burundi, 1999–2000.*

2001

24. Filip Reyntjens, *Again at the Crossroads: Rwanda and Burundi, 2000–2001.*

25. Henning Melber, *The New African Initiative and the African Union. A Preliminary Assessment and Documentation.*

2003

26. Dahilon Yassin Mohamoda, *Nile Basin Cooperation. A Review of the Literature.*

2004

27. Henning Melber (ed.), *Media, Public Discourse and Political Contestation in Zimbabwe.*

28. Georges Nzongola-Ntalaja, *From Zaire to the Democratic Republic of the Congo.* (Second and Revised Edition)

2005

29. Henning Melber (ed.), *Trade, Development, Cooperation – What Future for Africa?*
30. Kaniye S.A. Ebeku, *The Succession of Faure Gnassingbe to the Togolese Presidency – An International Law Perspective.*
31. J.V. Lazarus, C. Christiansen, L. Rosendal Østergaard, L.A. Richey, Models for Life – Advancing antiretroviral therapy in sub-Saharan Africa.

2006

32. Charles Manga Fombad & Zein Kebonang, *AU, NEPAD and the APRM – Democratisation Efforts Explored.* (Ed. H. Melber.)
33. P.P. Leite, C. Olsson, M. Schöldtz, T. Shelley, P. Wrange, H. Corell and K. Scheele, *The Western Sahara Conflict – The Role of Natural Resources in Decolonization.* (Ed. Claes Olsson)

2007

34. Jassey, Katja and Stella Nyanzi, *How to Be a "Proper" Woman in the Times of HIV and AIDS.*
35. M. Lee, H. Melber, S. Naidu and I. Taylor, *China in Africa.* (Compiled by Henning Melber)
36. Nathaniel King, *Conflict as Integration. Youth Aspiration to Personhood in the Teleology of Sierra Leone's 'Senseless War'.*

2008

37. Aderanti Adepoju, *Migration in sub-Saharan Africa.*
38. Bo Malmberg, *Demography and the development potential of sub-Saharan Africa.*
39. Johan Holmberg, *Natural resources in sub-Saharan Africa: Assets and vulnerabilities.*

40. Arne Bigsten and Dick Durevall, *The African economy and its role in the world economy.*
41. Fantu Cheru, *Africa's development in the 21st century: Reshaping the research agenda.*

2009

42. Dan Kuwali, *Persuasive Prevention. Towards a Principle for Implementing Article 4(h) and R2P by the African Union.*
43. Daniel Volman, *China, India, Russia and the United States. The Scramble for African Oil and the Militarization of the Continent.*

2010

44. Mats Hårsmar, *Understanding Poverty in Africa? A Navigation through Disputed Concepts, Data and Terrains.*

2011

45. Sam Maghimbi, Razack B. Lokina and Mathew A. Senga, *The Agrarian Question in Tanzania? A State of the Art Paper.*
46. William Minter, *African Migration, Global Inequalities, and Human Rights. Connecting the Dots.*
47. Musa Abutudu and Dauda Garuba, *Natural Resource Governance and EITI Implementation in Nigeria.*
48. Ilda Lindell, *Transnational Activism Networks and Gendered Gatekeeping. Negotiating Gender in an African Association of Informal Workers.*

2012

49. Terje Oestigaard, *Water Scarcity and Food Security along the Nile. Politics, population increase and climate change.*
50. David Ross Olanya, *From Global Land Grabbing for Biofuels to Acquisitions of AfricanWater for Commercial Agriculture.*

2013

51. Gessesse Dessie, *Favouring a Demonised Plant. Khat and Ethiopian smallholder enterprise.*

52. Boima Tucker, *Musical Violence. Gangsta Rap and Politics in Sierra Leone.*

53. David Nilsson, *Sweden-Norway at the Berlin Conference 1884–85. History, national identity-making and Sweden's relations with Africa.*

54. Pamela K. Mbabazi, *The Oil Industry in Uganda; A Blessing in Disguise or an all Too Familiar Curse? Paper presented at the Claude Ake Memorial Lecture.*

55. Måns Fellesson & Paula Mählck, *Academics on the Move. Mobility and Institutional Change in the Swedish Development Support to Research Capacity Buildiing in Mozambique.*

56. Clementina Amankwaah. *Election-Related Violence: The Case of Ghana.*

www.ingramcontent.com/pod-product-compliance
Lightning Source LLC
Chambersburg PA
CBHW080209300326
41934CB00039B/3435